Piano • Vocal • Guitar

BRANDON HEATH LEAVING EDEN

ISBN 978-1-61780-359-8

7777 W. BLUEMOUND RD. P.O. BOX 13819 MILWAUKEE, WI 53213

LEAVING EDEN

Words and Music by BRANDON HEATH
and LEE THOMAS MILLER

F
Am7
I just waved to a stran - ger; he did - n't wave back.
G
F
(One more step a - way.) And if it weren't for my T -
Am7
G
- V, I would - n't know what is real.
F
Am7
(One more step a - way.) My doc - tor can't do a thing for how I feel.

G
F
Feels like I'm leav - in'
C
G
F
E - den.
Feels like I'm leav - in'
C
G
F
E - den.
Peo - ple are los - ing their homes
Am7
G
to hur - ri - canes.
(One more step a - way.)

F
Am7
G
Old la-dy liv-ing next door for-got her own name.
F
Am7
(One more step a-way.) Teach-er is hid-ing her Bi - ble, but at least she's got a
G
F
job. (One more step a-way.) My lo-cal Sal-va-tion Ar -
Am7
G
- my just got robbed. Oh, feels like I'm leav-

F
C
G
- in' E - den.
f
F
C
Feels like I'm leav - in' E -
G
F
- den. Oh, it's like I'm fur - ther a - way
C
G
with ev - 'ry step I take. And I can't go back, 'cause I'm leav -

F
C
G
- in' E - den.
Dm
Am7
I'm go - ing, go - ing home.
mp
G
Dm
I'm go - ing,
Am7
G
Dm
go - ing home. There's no place,
mf

Am7
G
no place like home.
Oh, there's no
Dm
Am7
G
place, no place like home, home, oh,
cresc.
Fmaj7
C
when you're leav - in' E -
f
G
Am
F
- den, when you're leav - in'

C
G
Am7
E - den.
Oh,
F
C
G
it's like I'm fur-ther a-way with ev-'ry step I take.
And I can't
Am7
F
C
go back, 'cause I'm leav - in',
leav -
F
C
G
in'
E - den.

YOUR LOVE

Words and Music by BRANDON HEATH
and JASON INGRAM

Bm
G
D
I tried to sat - is - fy the hun - ger; I nev - er got it right,
I nev - er got it right.
3
So I climbed a moun - tain, built an al - tar,
You know the ef - fort I have giv - en,
looked out as far as I could see.
You know ex - act - ly what it cost.

Bm G D
And ev - 'ry day ___ I'm get - ting old - er, I'm run - ning out ___ of dreams, _
And though my in - no - cence was tak - en, not ev - 'ry - thing _ is lost, ___
Bm G D
___ I'm run - ning out of dreams. _
___ not ev - 'ry - thing is lost. ___ But Your
G D Bm A
love, Your love, the on - ly thing _ that mat - ters is ___ Your
G D Bm A
love. Your love is all I have _ to give. _ Your

G
D
Bm
A
love is e - nough to light up the dark - ness. It's Your
To Coda
1
love, Your love.
All I ev - er need - ed is Your love.
Gmaj7
2
All I ev - er need - ed is Your love.
You're the hope in the morn-ing,

A
Bm
G
D
A
Bm
You're the light when the night is fall-ing, You're the song when my heart is sing-ing. It's Your love.
G
D
A
Bm
You're the eyes to the blind man, You're the feet to the lame man walk - ing,
G
D
A
You're the sound of the peo - ple sing - ing. It's Your love, Your
G
D
Bm
A
G
D
love, Your love.

Bm
A
D.S. al Coda
CODA
But Your
All I ev - er need - ed is Your
G
D
love.
All I ev - er need - ed is Your
love, Your love.
All I ev - er need - ed is Your love.
1
2
It's all I ev - er need - ed.

THE LIGHT IN ME

Words and Music by BRANDON HEATH
and DANIEL MUCKALA

Moderate Rock beat

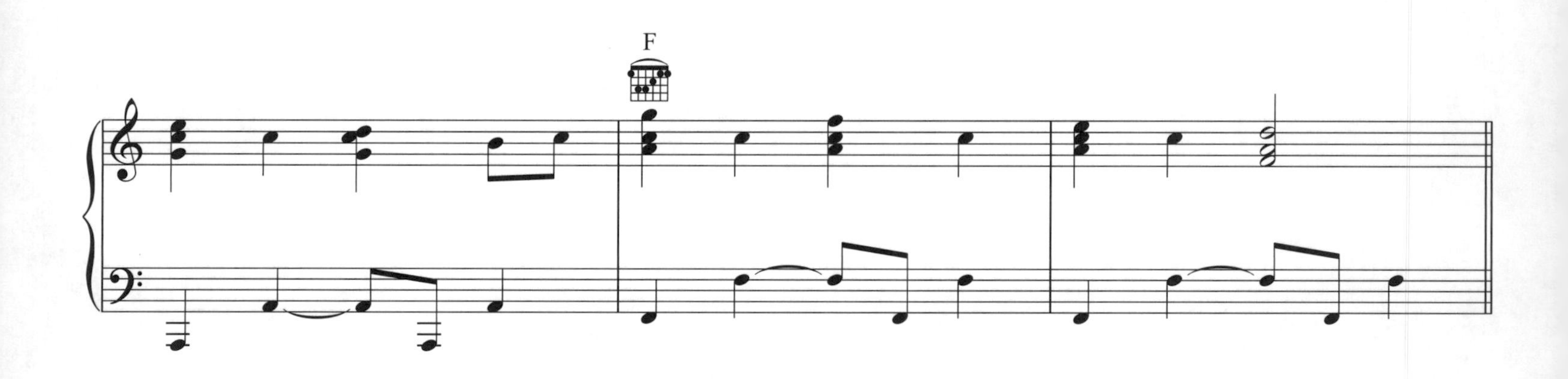

Fmaj7
I was a flame burn-ing down.
I was burn - ing out,
C
but You knew me bet - ter.
Am7
For
Fmaj7
You there was nev - er a doubt,
not since You gave me life.
G
Am
F
Some-thing was dif - f'rent; I knew it the in - stant

C
You put the light in me, the spark, the shot to the heart. You are the
Am
F
hope that leads me out of the dark. You let Your love shine down
G
so that the world could see You put the light in me,
F
Am
C
the light. You put the light in me, the light.

G
F
Am
You put the light in me, the light. You put the light in me,
C
To Coda
G
C
the light. You put the light in me.
Am7
You are the Mak - er,
You tell the sun when to rise.
Fmaj7
C
I'm just a house on a hill, but

Am7
You make me bright - er
than all the stars in the sky.
Fmaj7
Keep me from grow - ing
G
dim.
'Cause in Your per - fec -
Am
tion I'm just a re - flec -
F
tion,
so pull me clos -
C
er to You.
G
I'll catch like a fi -
Am
re
and I'll hold You high -
F
er,
'cause

D.S. al Coda
CODA
G
You put the light in me,
You put the light in me.
F
Am
I'll raise it high, I'll let it show
C
G
F
from the roof - tops down to the streets be - low. In day and night
Am
C
G
You will be known, and all will see

C
You put the light in me.
Am7
F
'Cause
C
You put the light in me, the spark, the shot to the heart. You are the
Am
F
hope that leads me out of the dark. You let Your love shine down

G
so that the world could see You put the light in me,
F Am C
the light. You put the light in me, the light.
G F Am
You put the light in me, the light. You put the light in me,
C G Fmaj7
the light. You put the light in me.

ONLY WATER

Words and Music by BRANDON HEATH,
ROSS COPPERMAN and LEE THOMAS MILLER

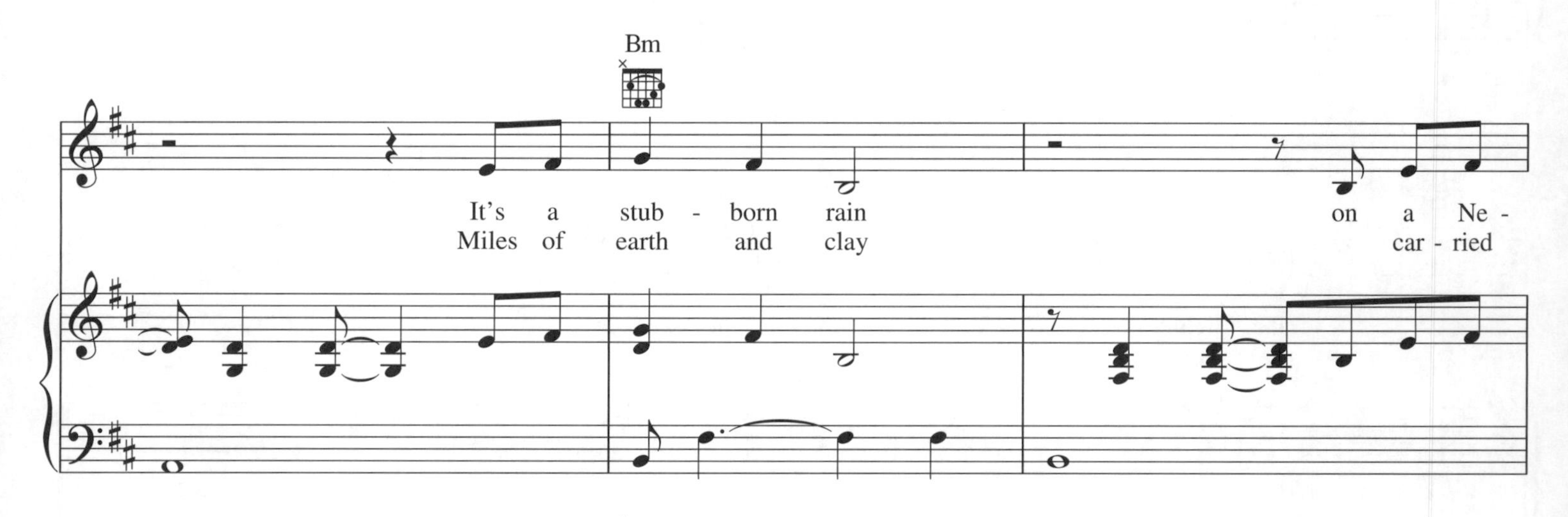

G
D
bras - ka plain. There's a farm - er stand - ing
far a - way. But there's some - thing ho - ly
A7sus
on a thirst - y ground. He
in these ca - the - dral walls. They took a
Bm
G
holds his breath; this is life or death.
lot of years and a lot of tears.
A7sus
Play 1st time only
D5
5fr
It's on - ly wa - ter. And it

Play 2nd time only
D5
5fr
Bm
And it wash - es
G
Bm
G
o - ver me like a sin - gle riv - er stone; chang - es
Bm
G
Em7
ev - 'ry - thing, but has no pow - er on its own.
G
A7sus
1
D5
5fr
It's on - ly wa - ter. There's a

2
D5
5fr
Bm
Oh,
Gmaj7
Bm
G
ooh.
Oh,
mf
Bm
Gmaj7
Em7
oh.
dim.
D
There once was a wed-ding.
All the
mp

A7sus
wine was gone.
They said, "He's
Bm
G
just a man."
That's where it all be - gan.
N.C.
It was on - ly wa - ter.
And it
mf
Bm
G
wash - es o - ver me like a

Bm
G
sin - gle riv - er stone; changes - es
Bm
G
ev - 'ry - thing, but has no pow - er
1
Em7
on its own. It
2
Em7
on its own,
G
on its own. It's on - ly wa - ter.

STOLEN

Words and Music by BRANDON HEATH,
DANIEL MUCKALA and NATE CAMPANY

* Recorded a half step lower.

Am
C
Dm7
luck - y if I make it through the night. But I
F
Am
C
can't sleep knowing that You're one more step a - head
F
Am
G
of me. I'm a fool for ev - er think - ing You'd just let
F
Am
C
me go. That's not the way it's ev - er gone be - fore.

Dm7
Fmaj7
C
I'm Yours.
You catch me like a thief in the night.
G
Am7
F
You hold me when I put up a fight.
You
C/E
G
Am7
chase me when I run from Your light.
Be - cause You love,
You won't give up
Dm7
F
Am
C
'til my heart is sto - len,
'til my heart is

To Coda
F
Am7
C/G
F
sto - len a - way. I'm try - ing to
Am
C
F
un - der - stand that life comes af - ter dy - ing, to em - brace
Am
G
F
that I'm a slave un - til I'm cap - tured. But You would
Am
C
Dm7
F
D.S. al Coda
nev - er use a lock or a key, 'cause I am free. You

CODA
Am7
C/G
F
Am
C
'Til my heart is sto - len.
My heart is
F
Am7
C/G
Dm
sto - len.
I could change my name,
cov - er all
Am
G
Dm7
my tracks,
but I'm wrong to think
I could lose
Am
Am/G
Dm
the past.
'Cause You found me here
and You took

Am
G
F
me back. Once a crim - i - nal, now a prod -
- i - gal. You catch me like a thief in the night.
C
G
Am7
You hold me when I put up a fight.
F
C/E
You chase me when I run from Your light.

G
Am7
Dm7
Be - cause You love, You won't give up 'til my heart is
F
Am
C
F
sto - len, 'til my heart is sto - len a - way,
Am7
C/G
F
Am
C
'til my heart is sto - len, my heart is
F
Am
C/G
Fmaj7
sto - len.

MIGHT JUST SAVE YOUR LIFE

Words and Music by
BRANDON HEATH

* Recorded a half step lower.

Am
G
safe anymore. Uh-huh, uh-huh, yeah.
Dm
Am
I know you thought
G
Dm
your faith was gone, but I'm as re-al as the fi-re that you're on.
Am
Am/G
Dm
I'm not a-fraid, know how to fight, and I ain't leav-ing here a-

Am
G
lone to - night. Uh - huh, uh - huh, yeah.
Dm
Am
It might just save your life. Uh -
G
Dm
huh, oh, yeah. It might just save you.
C
G
Dm
Just be - cause you give up on your - self

C
G
does - n't mean that I gave up my - self,
Dm
F
my - self,
Am
G
oh.
Dm
Am
Might just save your life, yeah.

G
Dm
N.C.
Don't be a - fraid,
stand up and fight,
'cause I ain't leav - ing here a -
Dm
Am
G
lone to - night. Uh - huh,
uh - huh,
uh -
Dm
Am
huh.
It might just save your life.
Uh -

G
Dm
huh, uh - huh. It might just save your life.
Am
G
Dm
Uh - huh, uh - huh. It
Am
G
might just save your life. Uh - huh, uh -
Dm
Am
huh. It might just save your life.

IT'S ALRIGHT

Words and Music by BRANDON HEATH,
THAD COCKRELL and MICHAEL LOGAN

Fm
B♭
B♭sus
Soon as He o - pens His eyes, the storm just
B♭
E♭(add2)
6fr
E♭/G
3fr
dies. "It's al - right.
Fm7
B♭sus
B♭
E♭(add2)
6fr
Ev - 'ry - thing - 'll be o - kay. You just hold
E♭/G
3fr
Fm7
B♭sus
B♭
tight. I'll be with you the whole way.

A♭sus2
3fr
B♭
A♭/C
When you're weak, I'll be strong.
Keep go - ing; we're al -
B♭/D
E♭(add2)
6fr
E♭/G
3fr
- most home. It's al - right.
Fm7
B♭sus
E♭
3fr
Ev - 'ry - thing - 'll be o - kay."
Gm/D
E♭/A♭
6fr
A♭6/9

E♭
Gm/D
E♭/A♭
3fr
6fr
Moth - er Mar - y's got a bro - ken heart from the words they're
mf
A♭6/9
E♭
Gm/D
say - ing. Her ba - by boy's be - ing torn a - part
E♭/A♭
A♭6/9
Fm7
by the world He's sav - ing. He says, "Moth - er, don't
B♭
cry for Me. You know where I'll be. It's al -

E♭sus(add2)
E♭/G
Fm7
right. Ev - 'ry - thing - 'll be o -
B♭sus
B♭
E♭sus(add2)
E♭/G
- kay. You just hold tight.
Fm7
B♭sus
B♭
A♭sus2
I'll be with you the whole way.
When you're weak,
To Coda
B♭
A♭/C
B♭/D
I'll / He'll be strong.
Keep go - ing; we're / you're al - most home. It's al -

E♭(add2)
E♭/G
Fm7
6fr
3fr
right.
Ev - 'ry - thing - 'll be o -
B♭sus
A♭sus2
B♭sus
3fr
kay.
A♭/C
B♭/D
E♭
3fr
Ev - 'ry - thing will be o - kay."
E♭/D
E♭/A♭
A♭6/9
6fr
mp

E♭
Gm/D
E♭/A♭
No prom - ise of an eas - y road, just a des - ti -
A♭6/9
E♭
Gm/D
na - tion. Next time you for - get your hope,
E♭/A♭
A♭6/9
Fm7
Some - bod - y's wait - ing. Soon as you
B♭
B♭sus
B♭
D.S. al Coda
o - pen your eyes, you re - al - ize it's al -
mf

CODA
B♭/D
A♭sus2
3fr
B♭
- most home.
When you're weak,
He is strong.
A♭/C
B♭/D
E♭(add2)
6fr
Keep go - ing; you're al - most home. It's al -
E♭/G
3fr
Fm7
B♭sus
E♭
3fr
right.
Ev - 'ry - thing - 'll be o - kay.
mp
Gm/D
E♭/A♭
6fr
A♭6/9
E♭
3fr
rit.
8vb

IT'S NO GOOD TO BE ALONE

Words and Music by BRANDON HEATH, JASON INGRAM and DANIEL MUCKALA

* Recorded a half step lower.

A
Bm
-'ry-bod-y's sing-ing, but some-thing's wrong, 'cause you're miss - ing. Hey, hey, are you lis-
A
G
D
A
-t'ning? It's no good to be a-lone. It's no good
G
D
A
Bm
to be out there on your own. It's no good
G
D
A
Bm
for you an-y more than it is for me. It's no good,

G
D
A
G
D
no good for you to be a - lone,
oh, oh, a - lone.
A
Bm
G
D
To Coda
Oh, oh, a - lone,
oh, oh, a - lone.
A
G
No good to be a - lone.
It's been
D
A
a lit-tle while, you've been out-ta the scene. Spend - ing all your time chas-ing down a dream takes a life -

Bm
A
- time. Ooh, it's a short life. You know,
D
A
it does-n't mat-ter how high you climb if no one's there to share the ride when you get
Bm
A
D.S. al Coda
there. Who's gon-na be there? It's no good
CODA
A
G
D
No good to be a-lone. No-bod-y's sup-posed to be an is-

A
Bm
G
D
- land,
stuck out in the mid - dle of the o -
- cean on your own.
I'm not giv - ing up un - til I find
you.
Give me an S. O. S., I'll bring you home.
It's no good for you to be a - lone.

A
Bm7
A
G
D
It's no good to be a - lone.
A
G
D
It's no good to be out
A
Bm
G
D
there on your own. It's no good for you an - y more

A
Bm
G
D
than it is for me. It's no good, no good for you
A
G
D
to be a - lone, oh, oh, a - lone.
A
Bm
G
D
Oh, oh, a - lone, oh, oh, a - lone.
1
A
No good to be a - lone.
2
A
N.C.
No good to be a - lone.

NOW MORE THAN EVER

Words and Music by BRANDON HEATH
and JASON INGRAM

F♯m
D
Bm
I've been liv - ing in a for - eign land;
con - fes - sion of a
E
F♯m
D
bro - ken man. I want You now more than ev - er.
Bm
E
A
The more I see,
C♯m
4fr
the more I want. The more I know, it does - n't stop.
f

F♯m
A
D
Your beau-ty speaks to call me home,
now more than ev-er.
A
C♯m
4fr
The more I feel that You are here,
the more the world
dis-ap-pears.
F♯m
And all I want
A
is to be whole,
D
To Coda
now more than ev-er.
F♯m
mf
So tell me some-thing that I

D
Bm
E
have - n't heard; _ I'll be hang - ing on ev - 'ry word. _ I want _
F♯m
D
Bm
___ You, now ___ more than ev - er. __________
E
F♯m
D
How long must You make me wait? _
Bm
E
F♯m
Give me hope, give me strength. _ I want ___ You now _

D
Bm
E
D.S. al Coda
more than ev - er.
CODA
Dmaj7
C♯m
4fr
now more than ev - er.
I will
mf
D
B
keep my eyes o - pen,
keep my eyes o - pen,
D
A
face to the sky.
I will

E
B
keep my eyes o - pen,
keep my eyes o - pen
D
A
(for You.)
f
C♯m
4fr
F♯m
Dsus2(add♯4)

A
The more I see, the more I want.
C♯m
The more I know, it does-n't stop.
F♯m
Your beau-ty speaks
to call me home,
D
now more than ev-er.
A
The more I feel that You are here,
C♯m
the more the world

F#m
A
dis - ap - pears. And all I want is to be whole,
D
A
now more than ev - er.
C#m
4fr
F#m
I will keep my eyes o - pen, keep my eyes
Dsus2(add#4)
A
o - pen.

THE ONE

Words and Music by BRANDON HEATH,
JASON INGRAM and DANIEL MUCKALA

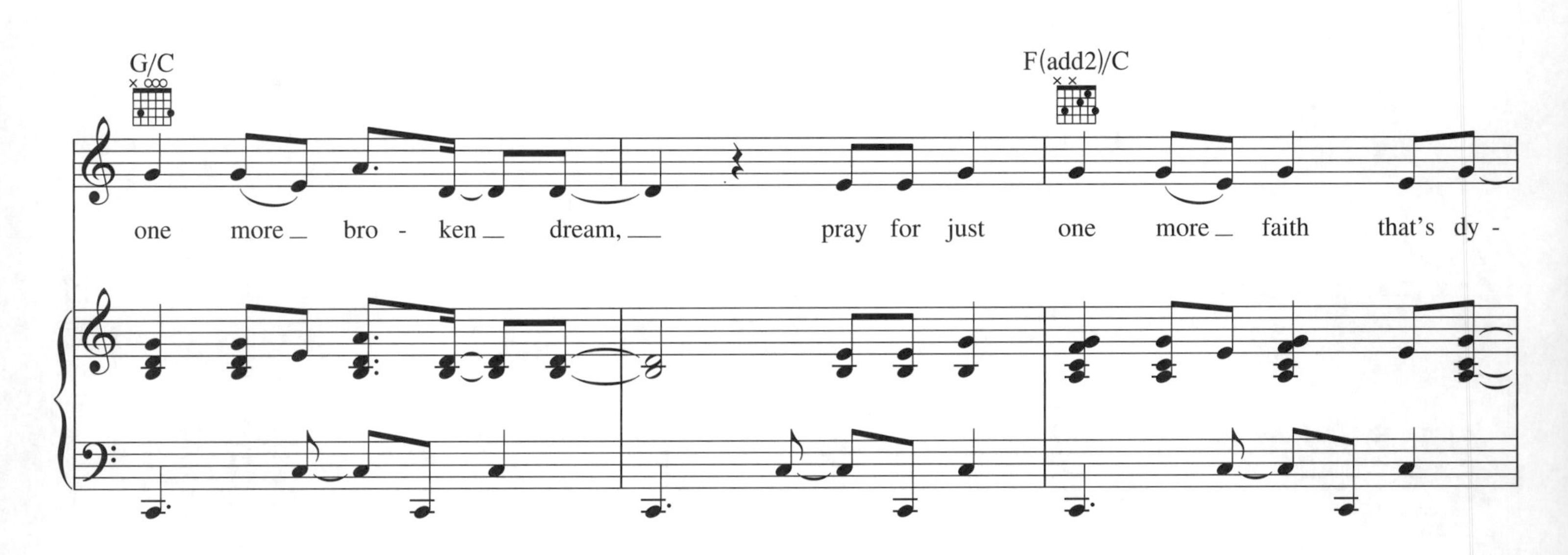

Fsus2
- ing, it's one too man - y. And if I see
C
G/C
one more child walk - ing just one more mile for wa -
F(add2)/C
- ter, if I wait one more min - ute long - er, it's one too
Fsus2
C
man - y. When I think of what could be

G/B
if we let our hearts be - lieve that it takes
Am7
Fsus2
just one, just one could turn this all a - round.
C
And if we're liv - ing his - to - ry, how will they think of
G/B
Am7
you and me? If it takes just one,

To Coda
Fsus2
Gsus
3fr
just one, what if, what if, what if I'm the one?
Csus2
3fr
G/B
It takes one, takes one, one.
Am7
It takes one, takes one, one. It takes one, takes
Fsus2
C
one. If I hear one more wid - ow cry -

G/C
- ing 'cause there's no one by her side, and if I see
F(add2)/C
one more fam - 'ly break - ing, it's one too man - y.
C
If there's one thing that I'm sure of, if there's
G/C
F(add2)/C
one thing that I know, you could be one in a sea of fac -

D.S. al Coda
- es or you could be one more chance for hope. When I think of
CODA
Gsus
3fr
C
what if I'm the one?
G
Am7
I see a na - tion with - out an - y walls, a
Fsus2
C
beau - ti - ful ha - ven for one and for all.

G
Am7
Fsus2
I see a day when peo - ple are free, when shack - les are bro - ken and
C
G
Am7
fall to the street. A voice, a cry, called out from on high, "The
Fsus2
C
G
first one of man - y, go lay down your life."
Fsus2
G
Ev - er think of what could be if we let our

Am7
G
Fsus2
hearts be - lieve that it takes just one?
G
N.C.
Just one could turn this all a - round. And if we're liv - ing
C
G/B
his - to - ry, how will they think of you and me?
Am7
If it takes just one, just one,

Fsus2
Gsus
3fr
C
what if, what if, what if I'm the one? (Oh, oh.)
C/B
(Oh, oh.) What if you're the one?
Am7
Fsus2
(Oh, oh.) (Oh, oh.)
1
Gsus
3fr
2
C
What if I'm the one?

AS LONG AS I'M HERE

Words and Music by
BRANDON HEATH

* *Recorded a half step lower.*

bet - ter than it was be - fore?
Of
all the things I've done, could I have done an - y more?"
C
D
G
Gmaj7/B
'Cause it took me a while just to find my feet, and to
mp
C
D
G
C
D
learn how to stand on my own. But You gave me the heart and the

G
Gmaj7/B
Em
Em/D
C
To Coda
time I would need to find You and make it back home,
G
Gsus
G
Gsus2
where I be - long.
Oh,
G
Gsus
G
Gsus2
G
Gsus
oh.
Some - day I'll go
G
D/G
G
Gsus
G
D/G
to the great wide be - yond,
where

G D/F# G Gsus
Mo - ses and Mar - y and Ja - cob and my loved ones have gone.
G D/G G C/E G/D D
But I will re - joice in to - day and the jour - ney I'm on,
G Gsus G D/G G
and I'll keep on pray - ing and
D/F# G Gsus G D/G
press - ing on un - til dawn. 'Cause it
D.S. al Coda
3fr

CODA
Cmaj7
D6
where I be - long.
mf
Em
D
Cmaj7
On - ly to see a
D6
G
Bm7
glimpse of Your face, to peek in - to heav - en, time and space. Oh, to feel
Cmaj7
D6
Em
my own frail - ty, to trem - ble in fear, to know You are with me as

D
Cmaj7
Gmaj7/B
long as I'm here,
oh,
as long as I'm
G5
3fr
here.
p
G
C/E
G/D
D
G
C/E
3
Some - day I'll pass
through the great sky a - bove,
G/D
D
G
C/E
G/D
D
G
3
and the first thing I'll ask
is, "How well did I love?"
rit.